SO-AFR-836

1ST Grade
Enjoying God's Gifts

by Cherie Noel

Positive Action Bible Curriculum

1st Grade: Enjoying God's Gifts

Written by Cherie Noel

Copyright © 1990, 2004, 2010 by Positive Action For Christ , Inc., P.O. Box 700, 502 W. Pippen, Whitakers, NC 27891. All rights reserved. No part may be reproduced in any manner without permission in writing from the publisher.

www.positiveaction.org

Third Edition, Revised 2010
Second Printing 2012

Printed in the United States of America

ISBN: 978-1-59557-062-8

Curriculum Consultant: Helen Boen
Editor: CJ Harris
Layout and Design: Shannon Brown
Artwork: Julie Speer

Published by

Contents

Lesson One
Day And Night

Use these words from Genesis 1:3 to fill in the blanks.
This is what God made on the first day.

God	light

_____ said, "Let there be _____,"

and there was _____.

Use these words to label the pictures.
These are things that were not here in the beginning.

| people | animals | flowers | rivers |

Label each picture with a word to tell what God made the third day.

hill	tree	lake	plant	flower

_____   _____   _____

_____   _____

God's Beautiful World

Make God's earth as beautiful as you can.
Finish the picture by drawing these things.

 hills and mountains

 Sun and Sky

a forest of Trees

Grass and Flowers

God's Gift: Four Seasons

Label the seasons.

| summer | winter | spring | fall |

_____

_____

_____

_____

Draw fish, birds, and other animals to complete the picture.

Use these words to label the pictures.
These are things for which we should be thankful.

| pets | trees | my home | good food |

I am also thankful for _____

_____

_____ .

Lesson Four
God Makes Man

Use these words to complete the sentences.

father	love	obey	mother

Adam was the first _____.

Eve was the first _____.

Mothers and fathers must love and _____ God.

Children must _____ and obey their parents.

God	family

✏️ _____ made the first _____ .

He made your _____ too.

✏️ _____ gave me my _____ .

Color the family in the picture below.

16

God gives everyone work to do. There is work for mothers and fathers. There is work for little boys and girls. When we do our work, we should always do our best.

 I work at _____.   I work at _____.

Use these words to complete the poem.

rest	might	right	best

I do my work

With all my ✎_____ ;

God is pleased

When I do it ✎_____ .

In all I do,

I do my ✎_____ ;

After I work,

Then I can ✎_____ .

Rules

Groups Need Rules

Write the correct numbers in the box beside each picture.

1. Raise hands for questions. 2. Line up for lunch.

3. Put trash in containers. 4. No running in halls.

Color the picture that shows a child obeying the rule about listening well in class.

Unit Two
God's Gift: Special Promises
Noah, Abraham, Jacob, And Joseph

Lesson Seven
Noah Builds An Ark

Use these words to answer the questions.

| Noah | ark | flood |

✏️ What kind of boat did Noah make? _____

✏️ What did God bring on the earth? _____

✏️ Who was God's friend?_____

Follow the dots to help finish the ark.

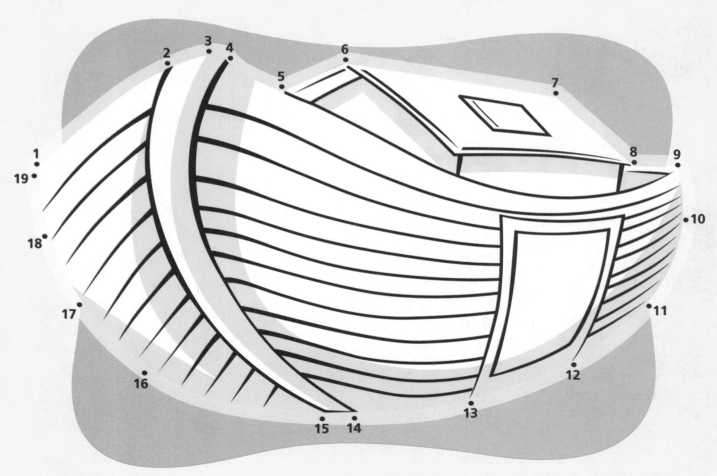

Write the correct numbers in the box beside each picture.

1. Noah prays and thanks God.
2. The animals go into the ark.
3. Noah builds an ark.
4. The Flood covers the earth.

Color the rainbow.

Red

Orange

Yellow

Green

Blue

Purple

God's promises are a special gift.

Fill in the blanks by unscrambling the words.

God promised in Genesis 9:11 that He would _____
ernve
again send a _____ to destroy the _____.
oodlf   rahet

Abraham Obeys God

This is how Abraham lived. Connect the dots then color to complete the picture.

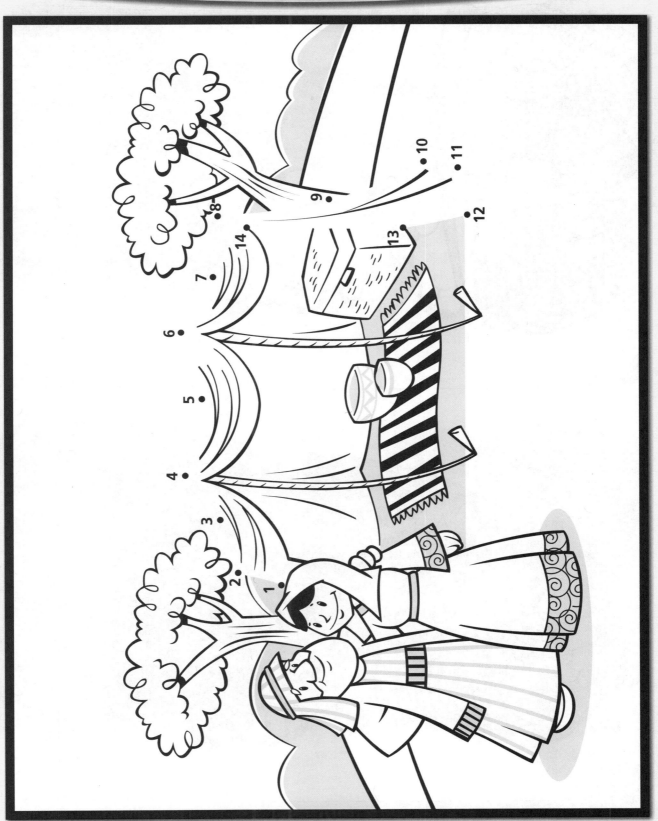

Use these words to answer the questions.

punished	blessed

✏️ God _____ Abraham because he trusted God.

✏️ God _____ Lot because he chose selfishly.

Lesson Nine
Jacob Has A Dream

These words state the promise God gave Jacob in Genesis 28:15.
Write them in the correct order on the steps of the stairway going up.

will	not	you	leave	I

5.

4.

3.

2.

1.

God's way is wise. When we choose our way, we are foolish. Under each picture write the word that describes the picture— either "wise" or "foolish."

Joseph Becomes A Leader

Write "**Jacob**" or "**Joseph**" below each picture.

_____   _____

Who confessed his sin?_____

Who forgave his brothers?_____

Number the pictures from Joseph's life in the correct order.

Head of Potiphar's house

Coat of many colors

Family moves to Egypt

In prison

Sold as a slave

Giving out food in Egypt

Lesson Eleven
Josiah—The Boy King

Draw the crown on Josiah's head to make him king.

Fill in the blanks below by unscrambling the words to learn what happened in 2 Chronicles 34:1-2.

Josiah was _____ years old when he became
gheit

_____. He did what was _____ in
kngi   tirgh

the eyes of the _____ and walked in God's _____.
droL   ysaw

Church is a gift from God.

Complete each sentence with one of these words.

pray	sing praises	listen

We _____ to God's Word.

We _____ and give thanks.

We _____ _____ to God.

Josiah Reads God's Word

King Josiah promised to obey all the laws of the Lord.

Number the pictures in the right order.

The idols are broken.

God's law is found.

Josiah is the king.

God's house is fixed.

King Josiah made a promise Like This one. can you make iT Too?

Use these words to make for yourself the same promise David made in Psalm 119:11.

sin	Word	heart

Lord, I will hide your _____

in my _____ so that

I will not _____ against You.

Lesson Thirteen
Joash—The Boy Who Forgot God

When Joash grew up, he forgot to serve the Lord. We need to serve the Lord now and stay faithful for the rest of our lives.

Use these words to complete the promise.

life	right	Lord	eyes	days

My promise to God:

I will do _____ in the _____ of

the _____ all the _____ of

my _____ .

_____
your name here

Do you serve idols or The True God?

In 1 Thessalonians 1:9, Paul says that he is glad to hear about people who turned to God from idols to serve the living and true God.

Circle the pictures that show how we worship the one true God.

Who am I?

Write the correct name below each picture.

| Adam & Eve | Noah | Abraham | Jacob | Joseph | Josiah |

Luke 1-2

The Savior is Born!

Mary's Gift From God

Use these words to complete the sentences.

angel	Jesus	joy	heart

Mary loved God with all her _____.

An _____ came to visit Mary.

Mary would have a baby named _____.

Mary sang a song of _____. Her baby

would be God's Son.

Fill in the blanks with these three words from Luke 2:46-49.

name	God	holy

✎Mary said, " _____ has done great

things. _____ is His _____."

Circle the words that mean "holy."

true   right   untrue

godly   sinful   perfect

Write the names of the three people to whom the angel appeared below the correct pictures.

Zacharias	Mary	Joseph

✎ _____   ✎ _____   ✎ _____

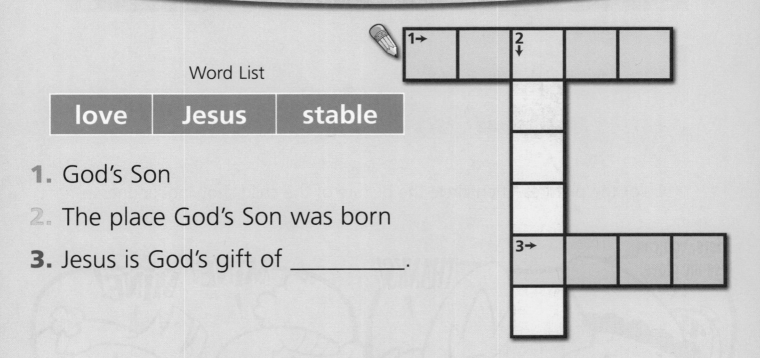

Word List

love	Jesus	stable

1. God's Son

2. The place God's Son was born

3. Jesus is God's gift of _____.

Connect the dots and color to see where Mary placed Jesus after He was born.

Use this code to complete the truth from Ephesians 4:32.

Code Box

a	b	c	d	e	f	g	h	i	j	k	l	m
1	2	3	4	5	6	7	8	9	10	11	12	13

n	o	p	q	r	s	t	u	v	w	x	y	z
14	15	16	17	18	19	20	21	22	23	24	25	26

| 2 | 5 | | 11 | 9 | 14 | 4 | | 20 | 15 | | 15 | 14 | 5 |

| 1 | 14 | 15 | 20 | 8 | 5 | 18 |

Color the pictures, then circle the picture of the child showing kindness.

The Shepherds And The Wise Men

Color the picture by number.

1	flesh
2	brown
3	light green
4	dark green
5	yellow
6	purple
7	light blue
8	dark blue

Bethlehem is the city of David. Who does Luke 2:11 say was born in that city?

A _____ who is Christ the Lord

Help the wise men use the Star of Bethlehem to find Jesus.

James 1:17 teaches us that every good _____ is from God.

The Boy Jesus

God wants us to grow up in many ways.

Write the numbers of the two items that apply to each picture in the boxes.

1 Read   **3** Praise God   **5** Go to church   **7** Write

2 Love   **4** Grow tall   **6** Grow strong   **8** Help others

Wisdom ☐ ☐

Stature ☐ ☐

Favor With Man ☐ ☐

Favor With God ☐ ☐

Learn To be Like Jesus.

Word List

share	obey	help	kind	work

Across:

1. Jesus liked to _____ in the carpenter shop.

4. Jesus liked to _____ what He had with others.

Down:

2. Jesus would always _____ His mother.

3. Jesus was good and _____ .

5. Jesus was a _____ to others.

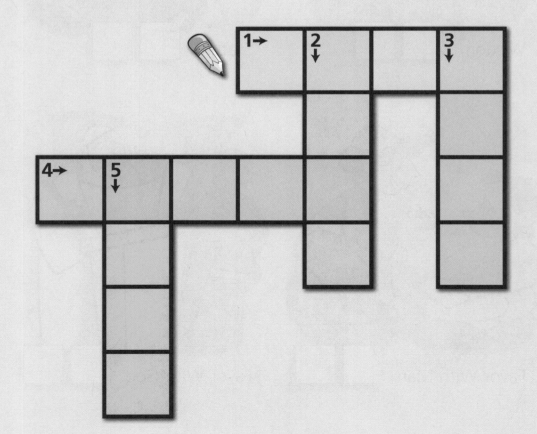

Jesus Is Tempted

Draw a smile on the faces in front of the sentences that are right.
Draw a frown on the faces in front of the sentences that are wrong.

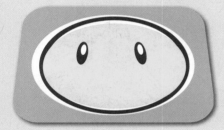 Satan is God's enemy.

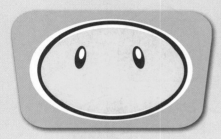 Jesus wanted to obey Satan.

 Jesus cannot sin because He is God.

 Jesus did not answer Satan.

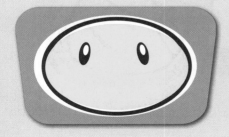 The Word of God helps us fight against Satan.

How God used angels...

Use these words to fill in the blanks.

Jesus	care	birth	dreams

In special _____

To tell Mary that _____
was going to be born

To tell the shepherds of Jesus'

_____

To _____ for Jesus

(and also for us)

Jesus Calls His Disciples

Jesus wants us to Learn from others. Where can we go to Learn?

Use these words to complete the sentences.
Then draw lines to the pictures that match the sentences.

church	home	school

I learn from my parents at

_____ .

I learn to read from my teacher at

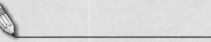
_____ .

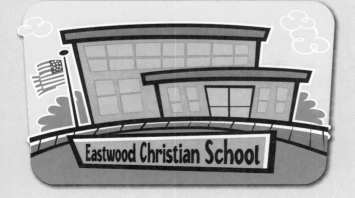

Eastwood Christian School

I learn more about Jesus in

_____ .

A disciple Learns To be Like Jesus.

Word List

love	joy	kind	obey

beoy

yoj

olve

nikd

Jesus Loves Children

Draw a smile on the faces in front of the sentences that are right.
Draw a frown on the faces in front of the sentences that are wrong.

 The disciples were glad to see the children with Jesus.

 Jesus wanted the children to come to Him.

 The children were afraid of Jesus.

 Jesus told the children never to be afraid.

 Jesus wants us to obey and love one another.

Jesus' words show us how much he cared about children.
In Luke 18:16, what does Jesus command his disciples to do?

Let the little _____ come to me.

Color those whom Jesus loves.

Number the pictures in the right order.

The disciples fed the people bread and fish.

"There is no food. We must send the people home."

There were 12 baskets of food left.

"I will share my lunch."

We must Learn To share what Jesus gives us.

What can boys and girls give To God?

Unscramble the words in the churches to fill in the blanks.

yots

I can share my _____ with friends.

lfse

I can give my _____ when I help others.

chchru

I can bring offerings when I go to _____.

rchose

I can do my _____ without being told.

Lesson Twenty-Two
Jesus Walks On The Water

In Matthew 14:25-27, what did the disciples think they saw on the water?

_____

Who was it really?_____

What did Jesus say they should not do? _____

Who made the sea and wind quiet? _____

Color the picture to match the small colored one.

Use these words to fill in the blanks.

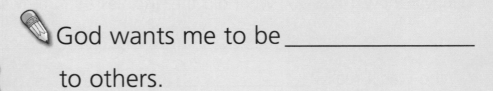

| share | courage | kind | wisdom |

✏️ God wants me to be _____ to others.

✏️ Jesus gives us _____ so we do not have to be afraid.

✏️ God wants us to _____ what we have.

✏️ When we learn, we have more _____.

Lesson Twenty-Three
Jesus Heals A Blind Man

Look up the verses and complete the quotations.

Jesus, _____
_____
_____
_____
_____ .

(Mark 10:47)

Go _____
_____
_____
_____ .

(Mark 10:52)

These are some ways we can show thankfulness to God.
Use these words to label the pictures.

giving	serving	thanking	singing

 _____

_____

 _____

_____

 Dear God, Thank You for _____

_____ .

Love, _____

The Lost Sheep

Use these words to complete the sentences.
Then draw lines to the pictures that match the sentences.

shepherd	sheep	cares	lost

One _____ was missing.

The _____ looked everywhere.

The shepherd found the _____ sheep.

Jesus also _____ for each of us.

Help the shepherd find the lost sheep.

Jesus is The Good Shepherd.

Word List

sheep	lost	saved	Jesus	cares

Across:

1. One sheep was ___ ___ ___ ___.

3. ___ ___ ___ ___ ___ loves each of His children.

5. The Good Shepherd ___ ___ ___ ___ ___ for each one of His sheep.

Down:

2. The shepherd loved every ___ ___ ___ ___ ___.

4. Jesus calls each person to be ___ ___ ___ ___ ___ .

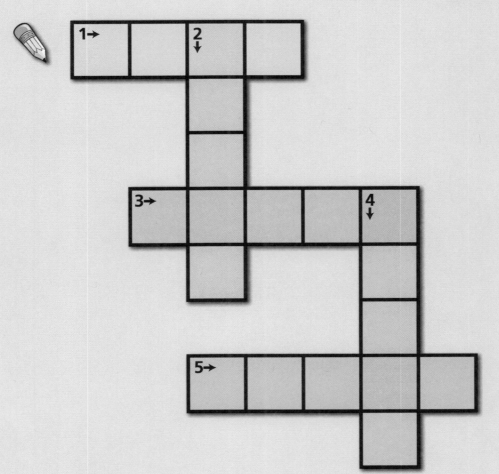

Lesson Twenty-Five
Jesus Is Crucified

Match the following questions with the pictures below.

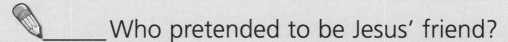_____ Who pretended to be Jesus' friend?

_____ Who took Jesus away?

_____ Who yelled, "Crucify Him!"?

_____ Who died on the cross for our sins?

_____ Who is Jesus?

A. Jesus

B. The People

C. God

D. Judas

E. Soldiers

God Sees Our Hearts.

Write the words in the correct column.

cheerful	proud	honest	wicked
good	joyful	foolish	fearful

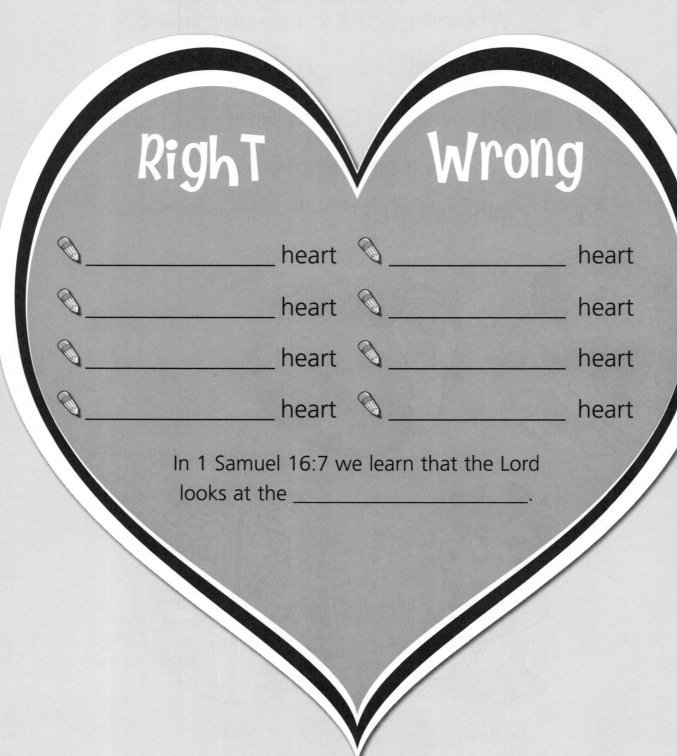

RighT

✎ _____ heart

✎ _____ heart

✎ _____ heart

✎ _____ heart

Wrong

✎ _____ heart

✎ _____ heart

✎ _____ heart

✎ _____ heart

In 1 Samuel 16:7 we learn that the Lord looks at the _____.

Lesson Twenty-Six
Jesus Lives!

Draw a smile on the faces in front of the sentences that are right.
Draw a frown on the faces in front of the sentences that are wrong.

 Jesus did not know what would happen to Him.

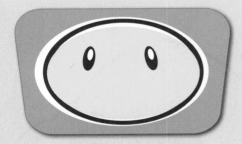 Jesus was in the tomb for three days.

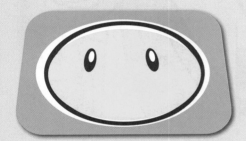 Jesus' promise came true. Jesus rose again.

 Jesus is God.

The Life Of Christ

Write the correct number in the box beside each picture.

1. Jesus cares for us.

2. Jesus rose again.

3. Jesus died on the cross.

4. God's Son was born.

OTTER PHOTOGRAPHY

FAMILY PORTRAITS
$10

Short Stories

Tessie

Use these words to complete the puzzle.

Elkanah	Samuel	prayed	child	son	faith

1. Hannah wanted a _____ (1 Samuel 1:11).

2. She _____ to God (1 Samuel 1:10).

3. Her husband was _____ (1 Samuel 1:8).

4. Hannah prayed for a _____ (1 Samuel 1:11).

5. She named her son _____ (1 Samuel 1:20).

6. Hannah had _____ in God (1 Samuel 1:18).

Samuel was a special gift from God.
You are a special gift too.

Tell how God made you special by filling in the blanks on the mirror.

✏️ I have _____ hair.

✏️ I have _____ eyes.

✏️ My birthday is _____.

✏️ I have _____ brothers and _____ sisters.

✏️ I like to eat _____.

✏️ My favorite game is _____ _____.

✏️ Something very special about me is _____ _____.

Lesson Twenty—Eight
God Speaks To Samuel

Begin with the S and circle every other letter.

Write the circled letters in the correct order to learn
how Samuel answered God in 1 Samuel 3:10.

_____ _____ _____ _____ _____ , _____ _____ _____

_____ _____ _____ _____ _____

_____ _____ _____ _____ _____ .

To Whom Does the Lord Want Us to Listen?

Use these words to complete the sentences.

| Bible | pastor | parents | teacher |

God wants me to listen to my

_____ .

God wants me to listen to my

_____ .

God wants me to listen to the

_____ .

God wants me to listen to my

_____ .

Who am I?

Write the name of the correct person below each picture.

| Abraham | Hannah | Joseph | Mary | Jesus | Samuel |

_____   _____   _____

_____   _____   _____

In your own words . . .

What is Samuel telling Jesse?　　What is Samuel telling David?

What was God's plan for David . . .

When he was young? _____

When he became a man? _____

What is God's plan for you now?

Use these words to label the pictures.

| play | listen | read | work |

 I can show responsibility by _____

_____.

82

Lesson Thirty
David And Goliath

Use these words to complete the sentences.

| Goliath | God | David | stones | one |

✏️ The shepherd boy who had courage to fight the giant was _____ .

✏️ David picked up five _____ for his sling.

✏️ He only had to use _____ stone.

✏️ David killed the giant, _____.

✏️ David was not afraid because _____ was with him.

Use this code to discover the truths about God in Isaiah 41:10.

 = A    = E    = I    = O    = U

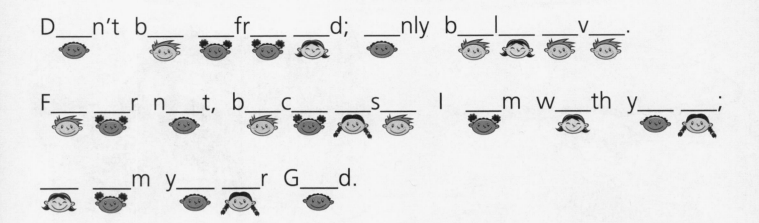

D___n't b___ ___fr___ ___d; ___nly b___l___ ___v___.

F___ ___r n___t, b___c___ ___s___ I ___m w___th y___ ___;

___ ___m y___ ___r G___d.

🖊 Who alone can take away your fears? _____

84

David And Jonathan

Word List

David	covenant	sword	love

Find 1 Samuel 18.

18:1 Jonathan loved _(3 down)_ in the same way he loved himself.

18:3 Jonathan and David made a _(1 down)_ because of their _(4 across)_ for each other.

18:4 Jonathan gave David his _(2 across)_ and robe to wear.

Unscramble the circled letters to complete the following sentence.

David and Jonathan were **f** __ __ __ __ __ __ .

Write the words in the box that tell how friends should act.

jealous   loving
rude   helpful
giving   unkind
kind   friendly

What other words can you think of that tell how friends should act? _____

_____

_____

God uses us in many ways.

Write the correct word to complete each statement.

| king | musician | friend | shepherd |

David was a...

Write the correct letter in the box beside each picture.

A. "This is all I have left."

B. "Cook some bread."

C. "Thank you for helping me."

D. "Would you give me some food?"

Use these words to answer the questions.

Elijah	the woman	God	the son

Who had a son that died?_____

Whom did the woman tell about her son?_____

Who laid himself on the boy and cried out to God?_____

Who came back to life?_____

Who made the boy live again?_____

God answers prayer.

Each picture shows a time to pray. Tell when you can pray under each picture.

_____   _____   _____

I can also pray when _____

_____.

Lesson Thirty-Three
Elijah Prays To God

Draw a smile on the face if the answer is yes or a frown if the answer is no.

 Did Baal answer the prayers of the people?

 Did Elijah pray to the True God?

 Did Baal send fire down on the altar?

 Did God send fire down on Elijah's altar?

 Is there only one True God?

Draw the fire on Elijah's altar.

Complete the prayer with these words.

God | **true** | **prayers**

Dear God,

I thank You that You are the _____ God. There is

no _____ besides You who can hear our _____ .

Acts 16:31 teaches that if we believe in the Lord Jesus, God will save us.

Choose the correct solution for reaching God from the words below and write it on the bridge that reaches to God.

| Going To Church | Serving Others | Trusting In Jesus |

GOD

Obeying Your Parents

Saying Prayers

In order for me to be saved, what is . . .

 My Responsibility? _____

 God's Promise? _____

God's Forever Gift: Heaven

Use the code to discover what Jesus said in John 14:2.

a	b	c	d	e	f	g	h	i	j	k	l	m
1	2	3	4	5	6	7	8	9	10	11	12	13

n	o	p	q	r	s	t	u	v	w	x	y	z
14	15	16	17	18	19	20	21	22	23	24	25	26

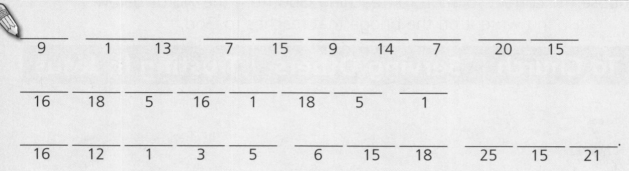

__ __ __ __ __ __ __ __ __ __
9 1 13 7 15 9 14 7 20 15

__ __ __ __ __ __ __ __
16 18 5 16 1 18 5 1

__ __ __ __ __ __ __ __ __ __ __ .
16 12 1 3 5 6 15 18 25 15 21

Let's Review

Write the name of the correct person below each picture.

| David | Josiah | Samuel | Jesus | Noah | Elijah |

_____

_____

_____

_____

_____

_____

God's Gift Of Forgiveness For Christians

In 1 John 1:9, we learn that if we confess our sins, we can trust God to forgive us.

Write what we should do in the spaces below.

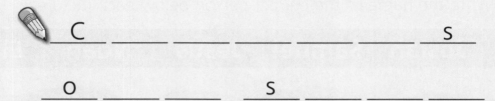

__ C __ __ __ __ __ __ __ __ s __

__ o __ __ __   s __ __ __ __ __

Write what God promises to do in the spaces below.

__ F __ __ __ __ __ g __ __ __ __ __   __ u __ __

Enjoying God's Gifts Scripture Memorization Report Sheet

Name:_____ Grade:_____ Teacher: _____

Week	Scripture	Due Date	Parent's Signature
1	Gen. 1:1		
2	Gen. 1:31a		
3	Eph. 6:1		
4	Eph. 6:2		
5	**Eph. 6:1-2**		
6	**Eph. 6:1-3**		
7	Gen. 9:11c		
8	Gen. 12:2a		
9	Gen. 28:15b		
10	**Review**		
11	Prov. 3:5		
12	Prov. 3:6		
13	**Prov. 3:5-6**		
14	Luke 1:49		
15	Luke 2:7		
16	Luke 2:11		
17	Luke 2:52		
18	**Review**		
19	Matt. 4:19		
20	Luke 18:16		
21	Eph. 4:32		
22	Matt. 14:27b		
23	Mark 10:52a		
24	John 10:11		
25	John 3:16		
26	**Review**		
27	Psalm 23:1		
28	Psalm 23:2		
29	Psalm 23:3		
30	**Psalm 23:1-3**		
31	Psalm 23:4		
32	Psalm 23:5		
33	Psalm 23:6		
34	**Psalm 23:4-6**		
35	**Psalm 23:1-6**		